MAXINE B. ROSENBERG

Living in Two Worlds

ILLUSTRATED WITH PHOTOGRAPHS BY
GEORGE ANCONA

Afterword by Dr. Philip Spivey

Lothrop, Lee & Shepard Books   New York

To Paul, who means the world to me—M.B.R.

To Joan Anderson—G.A.

1 2 3 4 5 6 7 8 9 10

Library of Congress Cataloging-in-Publication Data
Rosenberg, Maxine B.   Living in two worlds.
Summary: A photo essay about the special world of bi-racial children, who experience the advantages of two different cultures but sometimes face problems and prejudices.
1. Children of interracial marriage—Juvenile literature.   2. Parent and child—Juvenile literature.
[1. Children of interracial marriage]   I. Ancona, George, ill.   II. Title.   HQ777.9.R67   1986
306.8'46   85-23990
ISBN 0-688-06278-4
ISBN 0-688-06279-2 (lib. bdg.)

When people ask nine-year-old Toah which parent she looks like, she doesn't answer right away. Her face and nose are shaped like her mother's. The texture of her hair and the color of her skin are similar to her dad's. Toah hesitates before she answers the question because her mother is white and her father is black.

"I look like neither," she replies. "I'm biracial, a mixture of black and white. So's my sister, Amobiye."

Megan's father is a mixture of black and Cherokee Indian, and her mother is white. Seven-year-old Megan answers the same question this way: "I look more like Daddy, though I'm tan and cuter. Daddy and I both have curly hair and big teeth. My brother, Maceo, looks more like Mommy."

Many thousands of years ago, people lived in small groups that were geographically separated from one another. Each group developed some physical characteristics that were unlike any other group's. One of these differences was skin color. People in the Far East tended to have yellow-toned skin, and in the region that is now India, brown skin was most common. Europeans developed varying shades of light-colored skin, and on the African continent, skin tended to be dark. Other differences developed too—in the shape and color of the eyes, and in the texture and color of the hair. People in some groups were tall and thin; in others, short and stocky.

When scientists began to study the many ways human beings are alike, yet dissimilar, they referred to these groups of people as different "races."

Eventually, people began to move around and meet members of other groups. They married and had children who combined their parents' physical features. This is why, today, groups that are thought of as separate races include people with very different physical characteristics. For instance, not all people of African origin have dark skin, curly hair, and broad noses. People whose ancestors came from Europe are thought of as "white," yet their skin can be anything from the palest ivory to brown; their hair coloring ranges from blond to red and shades of brown and black, and they have every possible shape of nose. Each of these "races" is, in fact, a mixture of several differing peoples who created families together long ago.

Jesse's parents are of two different races, and so are
Shashi and Anil's. Jesse, seven and a half, has a mom
who is Chinese and a dad who is white. Shashi is eight
and a half and his brother, Anil, is seven. Their father
is Asian Indian and their mother is white.

How children look depends on how their parents look. If the mother and father are of the same race, all family members may closely resemble one another. Sometimes children clearly look more like one parent than the other. Mark has his father's nose and freckles; Isabel has her father's eyes and mouth.

Helga Ancona

In biracial families, where the mother and father look very different from each other, the children may not, at a glance, appear to bear a strong likeness to either parent. However, family resemblance will become apparent with a closer look, since all children—including biracial children—combine the physical traits of both their parents.

Shashi and Anil and their little sister, Divia, have their dad's black hair, dark eyes, and tan skin, though their skin is fairer than his. The boys are glad they resemble their father. "I wouldn't want to have hair like Mommy's," Shashi confides.

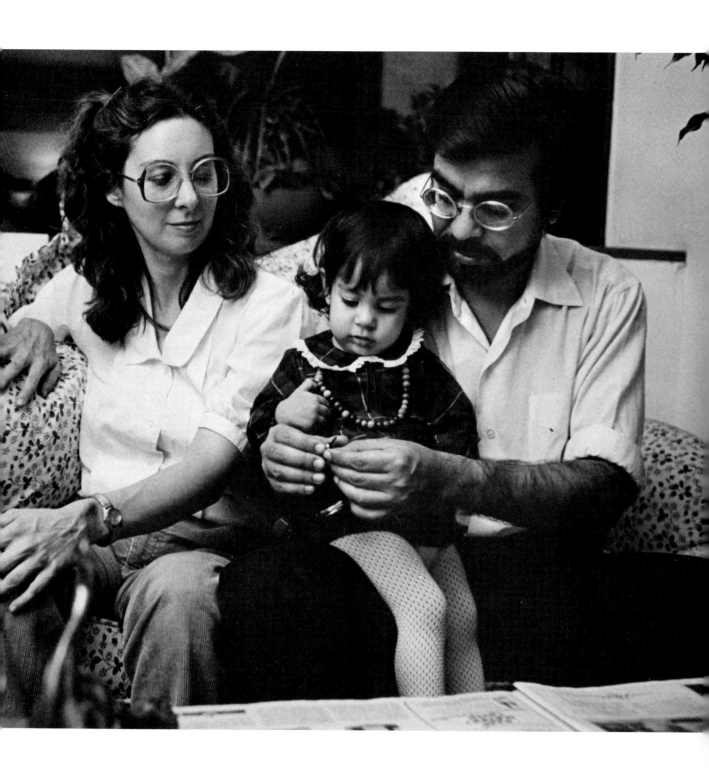

Jesse's sister, Emily, looks more like their mother than he does, even though they both have their mother's hair and skin coloring. From the day he was born, people noticed Jesse's strong resemblance to his father. "Everyone tells me I have my father's face," he says, "but that confuses me, because I also look Chinese."

In big and small ways, biracial children are reminded frequently that they look different from other children. They are often teased or asked embarrassing questions. Megan vividly recalls the time when she visited relatives who live in an all-white neighborhood. Before she left home, her cousin Tanya had braided her hair in cornrows, a style many black children wear. Megan thought the cornrows were great until children in her relatives' neighborhood told her she looked funny.

Anil doesn't like hearing, "Is that your father or your friend?" when people see him with his dad. "He's my father *and* my friend," Anil replies, but he wishes he hadn't been asked.

Like everyone else, biracial children don't like having to explain themselves.

Name-calling and remarks like "Your skin's dirty," "Your hair's dusty," hurt. Once when Megan told some children that her father is part American Indian, she remembers their response was, "Where are your feathers?"

It is not uncommon for some people of a majority race to cause people of other races to feel uncomfortable and make it difficult for them to fit into society. All over the world, there has been a long history of racial prejudice, which usually is expressed by trying to keep the races apart. For example, children of different races have been sent to separate schools, and people have had to live in separate neighborhoods. Certain jobs have been open to members of one race only. At the same time, however, many people of all races have worked hard to make certain that everyone is treated with fairness. Even so, there still are people who think they are superior to others because of the color of their skin.

Biracial children, especially those who are a mixture of white and black, see the effects of these attitudes in their daily lives.

When Megan visits Nana, her father's mother, she is aware that almost no white people live in her grandmother's neighborhood. She also is conscious that her mother stands out as different from most of the people around.

23

Societies Attitudes

When Megan visits her mother's parents, she realizes that there are very few blacks in the area where her mother grew up. "How did that happen?" she asks her mom.

Her mother explains that Megan's grandparents live in places where they settled a number of years ago, when segregation by color was a common practice. Although it is now illegal to refuse to rent or sell a home to someone because of his or her color, it takes a long time for neighborhoods to change. The fact that both sets of grandparents love Megan and welcome her into their homes is a sign that attitudes are not the same as they were only a generation ago. In time, more and more people will feel comfortable living in racially mixed neighborhoods.

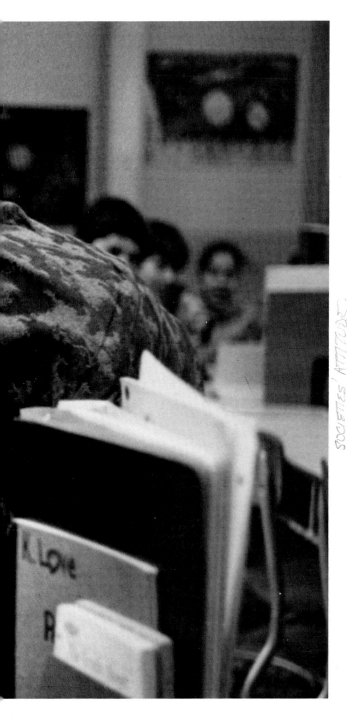

Toah thought that the teacher in her ballet class, where all the other students were white, went out of her way to be nice to her. "I guess she meant well, but she made me feel I was different." Even though Toah's white heritage is important to her, she feels she fits in better with kids whose coloring is more like her own. "I'm happiest when I don't stand out—like in school," she says. "I'm friendly with everyone, but my best friends are brown, like me."

In Jesse's family there are two languages, two religions, and two cultures. Because few Chinese live in his town, his classmates are especially curious about his background. "Say some words in Chinese," they frequently demand. Admitting he has trouble with the language, Jesse says, "I wish they'd stop pestering me. I don't even like it when Mommy and Aunt Yvonne want me to speak Chinese."

BOTH CULTURES

Living in a family with more than one cultural heritage can have extra benefits, though, such as more holidays. "We celebrate Hanukkah because Daddy and Grandma are Jewish and Christmas because Mommy is Christian," Jesse says.

"Then, on the Chinese New Year, Aunt Yvonne gives us red envelopes filled with money."

Shashi and Anil get special sweets to eat on Divali, the Indian New Year. "I love Indian food," Shashi says, licking his lips. "And my *nani* makes the best curried rice and *puri* [Indian bread]." At his grandmother's house, Shashi also enjoys playing with his cousins and hearing his father and grandmother speak Sindi, their native language.

33

Children who are brought up in two cultures tend to be especially sensitive to other people and their customs. And parents claim that through their children they gain a greater understanding of each other's heritage.

Although Toah and Amobiye's parents are divorced, their mother makes certain they learn about Africa and the importance of blacks in history. "Mommy reads about black people and then likes to tell us about them, particularly if they are women," Toah says.

Toah's mother heads an organization of families that have more than one racial heritage. "We go to meetings," Toah reports, "and grown-ups and kids talk about all kinds of things about being biracial—both good and bad. And we've made friends with a lot of different people."

Jesse, who knows a great deal about his Chinese heritage, is also interested in other Asian countries. He has been reading about Tibet and India, and he talks with his friend Jo-shin about Korea. Japan particularly fascinates him because his family lived there for three and a half years. "I met Takamiyama in Japan," Jesse says, beaming. Takamiyama is the Hawaiian-born 450-pound *sumo* wrestler.

Children who have learned to feel proud of their cultural heritage are often eager to share their traditions with others. Anil couldn't wait for Asian Week at school so he could wear the suit his dad had brought him from India. And Shashi delights in showing friends his collection of Indian comics. "One day I'm going to India to see the temples and cows," he tells them.

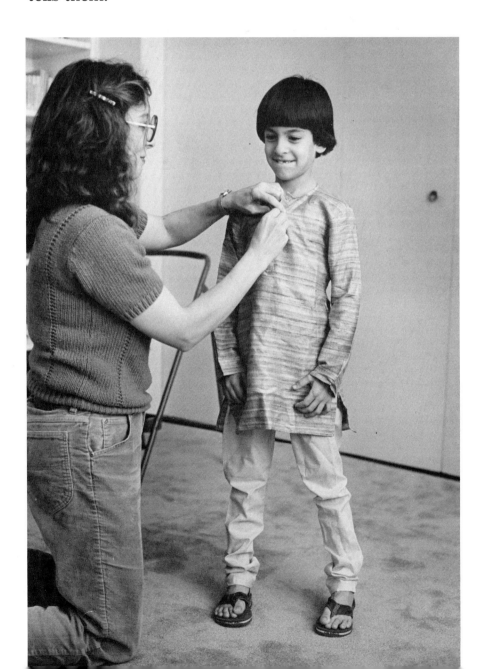

Jesse's friends like going to his home. Entering his house is like stepping into two worlds. First they take off their shoes; then later they eat hamburgers for lunch. "You're lucky," they tell him, as they play with his Chinese kites and his dinosaur collection.

"Yes, I am," Jesse agrees.

Many biracial children
feel the same way. Because
they have lived in mixed
families, they have learned
early that race is the least
important part of people.
And those who have lived
in neighborhoods with people of many different
cultures and gone to school
with them know that it is
possible to respect dif-
ferences and live
comfortably together.

Toah wrote in a poem:

Some people think
their opposites are bad.
I think all people
are the same
And everyone
should be friends.

Whatever their heritage, it takes time for people to become comfortable with the things that make them unique, and to be happy about how they look. "No one is pure white or pure black," Megan's teacher emphasizes, and Megan is careful to pick a crayon that matches her skin tone. The more children discover about themselves, the more they are apt to say that they wouldn't want to be anyone else.

"If I were born again, I'd want to be exactly as I am," says Anil. "Maybe six feet tall, though. And I'd want Mommy and Daddy to be the way they are, too. It would be boring if they were alike."

AFTERWORD

Traditionally, North American definitions of race have been limited primarily to notions of skin color and continents of origin. In recent years, however, racial differences have begun to be viewed in the broader terms of ethnicity and culture. At the same time, the social progress of recent generations, and especially the accomplishments of the civil rights movements of the 1950s, 1960s, and 1970s, has created a more positive climate for biracial living, making it possible for biracial families to exist in relative harmony with the culture at large.

Even so, some outdated notions and many stereotypes persist concerning the biracial child. Perhaps the most common misconception is that there are few biracial children in the general population and fewer still biracial marriages. The latest government statistics indicate that this is not so. In the 1980 United States census, over 600,000 biracial marriages were reported, and just under 2 percent of current births in this country are infants who could be classified as biracial—a significant segment of the population.

Biracial children also tend to be portrayed in popular literature as tragic heroes to whom life has dealt an unkind blow—as stigmatized, haunted, social outcasts of both cultures. The problem with these images is that they reinforce perceptions of biracial children that were never true generally and are even less true today. Recent research by several investigators of black-white biracial children found them to be socially competent, doing well in school, possessed of a clear sense of themselves, and not overly concerned or preoccupied with their racial identity. My own study of biracial teenagers reveals a psychological profile of children who have a robust self-image and carry on largely satisfying and constructive relationships with family and friends; they have acquired a keen social awareness that permits them to function successfully in many social arenas. As a rule, these children come from families where a premium has been placed on family sharing and multiracial living.

This is not to say that biracial families do not face special challenges. Typically, these families must try to secure surroundings that are compatible with biracial living. For the children, this means access to multiracial classroom settings, companions, and role models.

As a psychologist, I am particularly concerned with the healthy social development of children. As a person who also comes from a biracial family, I am especially gratified that *Living in Two Worlds* has so beautifully begun to deal with the benefits and challenges that come to children who have ready access to more than one world view. Biracial children are potential participants in the experiences, customs, joys, sorrows, accomplishments, and wisdom of two cultures. If concerned adults care to pass this heritage along to them over time, the children, in turn, will amaze us with the loving and wonderfully creative ways they combine the two.

PHILIP SPIVEY, PH.D.
Senior Psychologist, Department of Psychiatry
Bellevue Hospital Center, New York, New York